RACIAL JUSTICE IN AMERICA
HISTORIES

VOTING RIGHTS

KEVIN P. WINN with KELISA WING

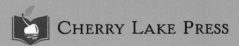
CHERRY LAKE PRESS

Published in the United States of America by Cherry Lake Publishing Group
Ann Arbor, Michigan
www.cherrylakepublishing.com

Reading Adviser: Beth Walker Gambro, MS, Ed., Reading Consultant, Yorkville, IL
Content Adviser: Kelisa Wing
Book Design and Cover Art: Felicia Macheske

Photo Credits: © Trevor Bexon/Shutterstock, 5; © Michael Scott Milner/Shutterstock, 6; Library of Congress/Photographer unknown, LOC Control No.: 2017894095, 10; National Archives/Commission on Civil Rights. Office of the Staff Director. 1957-(Most Recent). National Archives Identifier: 119652190, 13; Library of Congress/Photographer unknown, (1899?) LOC Control No.: 2001705854, 15; National Portrait Gallery, Smithsonian Institution/CC0/Photo by Sallie E. Garrity, Object No.: NPG.2009.36, 17; Library of Congress/Photo by Russell Lee, LOC Control No.: 2017738854, 19; Library of Congress/Photo by Warren K.Leffler, LOC Control No.: 2014645515, 22; Library of Congress/Photo by Thomas J. O'Halloran, LOC Control No.: 2018650324, 25; © Jamie Lamor Thompson/Shutterstock, 28; © Naresh777/Shutterstock, 30

Graphics Throughout: © debra hughes/Shutterstock.com; © Natewimon Nantiwat/Shutterstock.com

Cherry Lake Press is an imprint of Cherry Lake Publishing Group.

Library of Congress Cataloging-in-Publication Data
Names: Winn, Kevin P., author. | Wing, Kelisa, author.
Title: Voting rights / written by Kevin P. Winn, Kelisa Wing.
Description: Ann Arbor, Michigan : Cherry Lake Publishing, [2021] | Series: Racial justice in America: Histories | Includes index. | Audience: Grades 4-6 | Summary: "The Racial Justice in America: Histories series explores moments and eras in America's history that have been ignored or misrepresented in education due to racial bias. Voting Rights explores the regulations Black people and people of color have endured in pursuit of their right to vote. Concepts are approached in a comprehensive, honest, and age-appropriate way. Developed in conjunction with educator, advocate, and author Kelisa Wing to reach children of all races and encourage them to approach our history with open eyes and minds. Books include 21st Century Skills and content, as well as activities created by Wing. Also includes a table of contents, glossary, index, author biography, sidebars, educational matter, and activities"— Provided by publisher.
Identifiers: LCCN 2021010806 (print) | LCCN 2021010807 (ebook) | ISBN 9781534187467 (Hardcover)
  | ISBN 9781534188860 (Paperback) | ISBN 9781534190269 (PDF) | ISBN 9781534191662 (eBook)
Subjects: LCSH: Suffrage—United States—Juvenile literature. | Voting—United States—History—Juvenile literature. | African Americans—Suffrage—History—Juvenile literature. | Women—Suffrage—United States—History—Juvenile literature.
Classification: LCC JK1846 .W56 2021 (print) | LCC JK1846 (ebook) | DDC
  324.6/20973—dc23
LC record available at https://lccn.loc.gov/2021010806
LC ebook record available at https://lccn.loc.gov/2021010807

Cherry Lake Publishing Group would like to acknowledge the work of the Partnership for 21st Century Learning, a Network of Battelle for Kids. Please visit http://www.battelleforkids.org/networks/p21 for more information.

Printed in the United States of America

Kevin P. Winn is a children's book writer and researcher. He focuses on issues of racial justice and educational equity in his work. In 2020, Kevin earned his doctorate in Educational Policy and Evaluation from Arizona State University.

Kelisa Wing honorably served in the U.S. Army and has been an educator for 14 years. She is the author of *Promises and Possibilities: Dismantling the School to Prison Pipeline*, *If I Could: Lessons for Navigating an Unjust World*, and *Weeds & Seeds: How to Stay Positive in the Midst of Life's Storms*. She speaks both nationally and internationally about discipline reform, equity, and student engagement. Kelisa lives in Northern Virginia with her husband and two children.

CHAPTER 1

Who Can Vote in the United States?

Voting in the United States is an important right. When people have the chance to elect their leaders, it ensures that voices from all of the country's diverse communities are heard. It also holds our leaders accountable. When elected officials know they're being watched by the people they serve, they have to work for them. Voters have the power to remove elected officials from office if they aren't doing their job. It is important that our elected leaders serve their communities and that they're not in office simply because of the power it gives them.

About 160 million Americans voted in the 2020 election.

Voting in the United States has a long, dark history. When the country was founded, the signers of the Constitution only viewed certain people as important: White men. They believed they were the only people who should and could vote. This practice lasted for a long time. But many voting rights activists in U.S. history have worked to change this practice. These activists continue to do important work today.

Rallies around the country encourage people to vote, especially those who have had their voting rights restricted.

When we read history books, we might not think voting rights activists would have work to do today. Don't all people over the age of 18 have the right to vote? Weren't Constitutional amendments passed to ensure that people of any race or gender could vote? While these points are true, more and more restrictions are being put in place to limit voting rights. These restrictions often target specific voters, including Black people, the young, the elderly, and the poor. Many people in power work hard to make it difficult for these groups of people to vote and elect people to represent them.

United States residents are becoming more civically engaged. People saw this during the 2020 election. Candidates Joe Biden and Donald Trump each received the highest numbers of votes in a presidential election.

CHAPTER 2

The Fifteenth Amendment

Not everyone in the United States has always had the right to vote. It's been a long and uphill battle to achieve voting rights for all. When the Constitution was written, only White men could vote. After the Civil War, however, changes occurred. When the South lost the war, much of it was destroyed. It needed help, so the U.S. government gave the Southern states money if its leaders agreed to ratify the Thirteenth Amendment. The South reluctantly agreed.

The era when the North helped the South was called Reconstruction. During this time, the government sent federal troops to help rebuild and make sure the South didn't return to slavery. The U.S. government also passed two more amendments to the Constitution during this period. The Fourteenth Amendment made Black people U.S. citizens. The Fifteenth, importantly, gave all men the right to vote—a person's race couldn't be used to restrict their voting rights.

The Fifteenth Amendment states, "The right of citizens of the United States to vote shall not be denied or abridged by the United States or by any State on account of race, color, or previous condition of servitude." This meant that people couldn't be denied the right to vote because of their skin color. They also couldn't be denied voting rights if they had formerly been enslaved.

During 1865 and 1866, Black people held meetings around the South to advocate for themselves. They worked to ensure that they would have a say in government moving forward. They fought for the right to vote as well as against Black codes, which were racist rules put in place to maintain White supremacy in the South. Black codes targeted Black people, restricting them from jobs and from earning much money.

Hiram Revels served in Congress from 1869 until 1871.

With the new right to vote, Black Americans made huge gains during Reconstruction. Between the years 1870 and 1901, 22 Black people held office in the U.S. Congress. Two of them were Mississippi senators— Hiram Revels and Blanche K. Bruce. For the first time, Black Americans were represented in the government.

With the three new amendments, Black people made progress throughout society. Many made economic gains. They could start businesses. White people, especially in the South, resented seeing Black people making progress. They did everything they could to stop it. One way was through establishing Black codes. Black people could be arrested for breaking Black codes.

Black codes were the start of Jim Crow segregation—
a system of rules that kept Black and White people
separate, especially in the South. The attitude from many
White people was one of White supremacy—the false
belief that White people are better than all others.
White supremacy extended into voting. Because many
White people continued to think that they were better
than Black people, they believed Black people should
not vote. White people worked hard to find loopholes in
the Fifteenth Amendment. In the South, they succeeded.
From around 1900 through 1965, Black people were
blocked from voting. This was done through writing
racist laws or conducting racial terror lynchings—
harming and killing Black people who dared to vote.

In 1890, a committee of White people in Mississippi
met to rewrite the state constitution. The committee's
leader said that they were rewriting it "to exclude the
Negro." Mississippi and Louisiana also added a
"grandfather clause." This meant that all men could vote,
but only if a person's grandfather had been allowed to
vote. Because almost every Black man's grandfather
had been an enslaved person who couldn't vote, this
meant Black people still couldn't vote.

Governments, which are usually made up of White men, have used
many different tactics to try to keep people who may hold different
opinions from their own from voting.

CHAPTER 3

The Struggle for Black Women's Suffrage

The Fifteenth Amendment only applied to men. Women still were not allowed to vote, and they fought for the right. But even this fight was segregated. White women wanted the right to vote, even if it meant leaving out Black women. White leaders like Elizabeth Cady Stanton and Susan B. Anthony said that White women should have had the right to vote before Black men did. During protests and marches, some White women wanted the protesters to be segregated to appeal to Southern states. They told Black women to stand in the back during the marches.

Intersectional feminism means that the struggle for women's rights must bridge all other perceived differences.

Black women resisted White women's orders to stay in the back. They said they had as much of a right to vote as anybody else. Ida B. Wells-Barnett encouraged her fellow Black suffragettes to not stand in the back like White leaders wanted. She said if Black women "did not take a stand now in this great democratic parade then the colored women are lost." She predicted Black women would be excluded in any new amendment to the Constitution. Their work led to the ratification of the Nineteenth Amendment in 1920. This gave all women the right to vote.

Black women organized early to campaign for voting rights. One activist, Ann Shadd Cary, led a group of 60 Black and White women as early as 1871 to register to vote. She thought it was wrong that the Fifteenth Amendment excluded her because she was a woman.

Ida B. Wells was a journalist who exposed racial lynchings in the South. She also was a founder of the National Association for the Advancement of Colored People (NAACP).

CHAPTER 4

Working Toward the Voting Rights Act of 1965

Even with the passage of the Fifteenth and Nineteenth Amendments, Black Americans were continually excluded from voting through the 1960s. This was clear in the South. Former Confederate states found ways to skirt the amendments.

As White people were in charge of registering voters, they made up rules to prevent Black people from voting. White people enacted literacy tests and poll taxes. Potential voters were required to take a test to prove they could read. Sometimes, Black people had to recite the entire U.S. Constitution. Other times, Black people were forced to explain the most difficult sections of laws. Even when they had college degrees, White people told them they were illiterate and weren't allowed to vote.

They also used very tricky tests that had to be answered with no mistakes in short time limits. Sometimes, the questions wouldn't even make sense. White people graded the tests and decided whether or not a Black person passed. Even when Black people passed these tests, they were expected to pay an expensive poll tax. These tactics all kept Black people from voting.

PAY YOUR
POLL TAX-NOW!
Deadline January 31st

Vote! And Protect Your Rights and Privileges

Be Ready For Every Election---

Local Option and Other Special Elections are in Prospect for This Year

The poll tax was a way to keep Black people from the voting booths.

Many White people felt threatened by Black voters. In the late 1800s through the 1960s, Democrats ruled the South. However, in many ways, the political parties weren't the same that they are today. After slavery, many Black people would have voted Republican. The Southern Democrats didn't like that. Members of the Ku Klux Klan (KKK)—a White supremacist terrorist group—terrorized Black voters. They destroyed Black people's property or lynched them.

Maceo Snipes was a Black World War II veteran. He lived in Georgia, and he decided to vote. When the Ku Klux Klan found out, they shot him. Maceo walked for 3 miles (4.8 kilometers) and found a ride to the hospital. When he arrived, doctors told him they didn't have any "Black blood" for a transfusion. Snipes died 2 days later.

Throughout the 1900s, Black people continued to fight for the right to vote. They resisted White supremacy. This resistance led to a peaceful protest in 1964 in Selma, Alabama. On March 7, 1965, civil rights leaders like John Lewis, Reverend Hosea Williams, and Dr. Martin Luther King Jr., among others, marched peacefully for voting rights. When they reached the Edmund Pettus Bridge, Alabama state troopers met them. The troopers told the marchers to stop. They had 3 minutes to turn around. After only about 90 seconds, the troopers turned violent against the peaceful protesters. Many peaceful protesters were badly injured. The day came to be known as Bloody Sunday.

All of this violence was broadcast on national news. Americans around the country were furious. Many called for action. Something needed to be done about White supremacy, especially in the South. Black people still could not vote, even though the Fifteenth Amendment had passed almost 100 years earlier.

In the 1960s, many Americans organized to protest unfair voting practices. Together, they pushed the government to act.

Lyndon B. Johnson was the president of the United States at the time of the violence in Selma. He agreed that something needed to be done. In a speech after the violence, he said, "All Americans must have the privileges of citizenship regardless of race." With his help, Congress passed the Voting Rights Act of 1965.

Fannie Lou Hamer worked hard to secure voting rights for Black people. She was attacked by police for attempting to register to vote. She never fully recovered. Even so, she co-founded the Mississippi Freedom Democratic Party. After becoming frustrated with politics, she started a pig bank, raising money and donating pigs to Black farmers.

The Voting Rights Act of 1965 was essential. It held Southern states, and a few others, accountable. It forced them to follow the Fifteenth Amendment. The act said that states with a history of stopping Black people from voting couldn't change state voting rules without permission from the U.S. government. With the Voting Rights Act, states couldn't make voting difficult for Black people.

Because of the Voting Rights Act of 1965, many more Black people registered and voted. In fact, in 1964, only 7 percent of Black Mississippians were registered voters. Within 5 years, 61 percent of Black people were registered. Similar to the period after Reconstruction, Black people ran for office and won. The first Black senator since 1881 was elected in 1967. The first Black woman in Congress, Shirley Chisholm, was elected in 1968. Progress was being made.

Shirley Chisholm ran for president in 1972. Her campaign slogan was "unbought and unbossed."

CHAPTER 5

Voting Rights Today

Voting Rights remain an issue today. Although BIPOC—Black, Indigenous, and people of color—communities have gained access to voting, these rights are being stripped. Once again, rules and actions that make it difficult for Black people, the poor, the young, and the elderly are being put in place. This is because the Voting Rights Act of 1965 is losing power.

In 2013, the Supreme Court heard a case called *Shelby v. Holder*. The plaintiff said that the 1965 Voting Rights Act was no longer necessary. It had done its job. And now the government was overstepping on states' rights. The Supreme Court agreed.

Within hours of the Supreme Court weakening the Voting Rights Act, states put new voting restrictions in place that harmed groups of voters. This is called

voter suppression. New forms of identification are being required. Polling places have been moved. In fact, Texas closed many polling places so that there was only one place to drop off ballots in each county. This is a problem, especially because counties in Texas are huge. What are people supposed to do if they don't have a car to get to their polling place?

Other forms of voter suppression continue. For example, some states ruled that anyone with a criminal record isn't allowed to vote, even if they already served their time in prison. This rule has disproportionately affected Black people, who are targeted for crimes at a much higher rate than White people who commit the same crime. In fact, in Alabama, one-third of all Black men have been convicted of a crime. They were no longer allowed to vote. Although this rule is changing throughout the United States, it remains a significant problem.

Stacey Abrams is one of today's heroes of voting rights advocacy. People credit her with Georgia's voter turnout in 2020.

Other forms of voter suppression include requiring voters to present a valid residential address. Not every person has a permanent address. For example, this affects Native Americans living on reservations in North Dakota. States and counties control who gets residential addresses. Native American reservations are on federal land. Since they aren't officially part of the state or county, they don't receive addresses. Yet, the state requires an address to vote even though it is close to impossible for Native Americans to have one. Does this sound fair?

Today, activists are bringing attention to unfair voter suppression practices. One particularly important person is a Black woman named Stacey Abrams. She ran for governor in Georgia in 2018. She lost. Part of the reason she lost was that registered voters' names were suddenly deleted from the voter database. People whose names were removed didn't know they had been deleted from the system. When they went to vote, they found they were no longer registered. They couldn't vote on election day.

Abrams saw the injustice. And she fought it. She started an organization called Fair Fight. It works to make sure voting laws are fair and to fight voter suppression. The large Black voter turnout during the presidential and Senate races in 2020 and 2021 is attributed to her work.

Kamala Harris is the first woman and the first person of Black and South Asian descent to serve as vice president. She was elected partially in thanks to Abrams's work.

SHOW WHAT YOU KNOW

Do you know what an advocate is? An advocate is someone who fights for the rights of others. Congressman John Lewis was an advocate for civil rights and voting rights. Prior to his death in July 2020, he spent his life fighting and advocating for a more just America. After his death, the John Lewis Voting Rights Act of 2020 was introduced to restore the rules that were eliminated in the 2013 *Shelby v. Holder* Supreme Court decision. Specifically, the bill calls for oversight from the federal government on how states run their elections.

For this show what you know assignment, research why oversight is important. What happened before 1965 when there was no oversight for voting? How does oversight help to fight injustice in the country? Share why you think the oversight is important and how you can encourage other people in charge to have oversight and accountability.

Do you know there are so many different ways to show what you know? Rather than using traditional ways to display knowledge, try something new to complete this assignment. Here are some ideas:

1. Rap
2. Mural
3. Musical
4. Debate
5. Web page
6. Speech
7. Bulletin board
8. Jigsaw puzzle
9. Show and tell
10. Essay
11. Diorama
12. Performance
13. Podcast
14. Journal
15. OR add your own...

EXTEND YOUR LEARNING

Draper, Sharon M. *Stella by Starlight*. New York, NY: Atheneum/Caitlyn Dlouhy Books, 2016.

"The Civil Rights Act of 1964 and the Voting Rights Act of 1965." Khan Academy, www.khanacademy.org/humanities/us-history/postwarera/civil-rights-movement/a/the-civil-rights-act-of-1964-and-the-voting-rights-act-of-1965. Accessed January 31, 2021.

GLOSSARY

abridged (uh-BRIJD) something that is changed or shortened

advocate (AD-vuh-kayt) to support or work for

excluded (ik-SKLOO-duhd) left out, not included

Jim Crow segregation (JIHM CROH seg-ruh-GAY-shuhn) a system of laws that separated White people from other races, especially Black people

loopholes (LOOP-hohles) ambiguities or inadequacies in a law or rule

plaintiff (PLANE-tuhf) the person who brings a case to court

racial terror lynchings (RAY-shuhl TER-uhr LINCH-ings) violent attacks by White people on BIPOC, especially Black people, to scare and control them; usually done through torture, murder, and hanging

ratify (RAH-tuh-feye) to officially approve of something, such as a law

restrictions (ri-STRIK-shuhns) limitations preventing people from doing something

suffragettes (suh-frih-JETS) women who support or fight for women's voting rights

voter suppression (VOH-tuhr suh-PREH-shuhn) working to prevent people from voting

White supremacy (WITE suh-PREH-muh-see) the incorrect belief that White people and their ideas are superior to all others

INDEX